Pebble®
Plus

Goblin Sharks

A 4D Book

by Marissa Kirkman

CAPSTONE PRESS
a capstone imprint

Download the Capstone 4D app!

- Ask an adult to download the Capstone 4D app.
- Scan the cover and stars inside the book for additional content.

When you scan a spread, you'll find fun extra stuff to go with this book! You can also find these things on the web at www.capstone4D.com using the password: goblin.01570

Pebble Plus is published by Capstone Press,
1710 Roe Crest Drive, North Mankato, Minnesota 56003
www.mycapstone.com

Library of Congress Cataloging-in-Publication Data
Library of Congress Cataloging-in-Publication data is
available on the Library of Congress website.
ISBN 978-1-9771-0157-0 (library binding)
ISBN 978-1-9771-0161-7 (paperback)
ISBN 978-1-9771-0165-5 (eBook PDF)

Editorial Credits
Charmaine Whitman, designer; Kelly Garvin, media
researcher; Kathy McColley, production specialist

Image Credits
Seapics: David Shen, 5, 17, 19; Makoto Hirose/e-Photo, cover,
1, 7, 9, 11, 13, 15, 21; Shutterstock: Maquiladora, 8, Rich Carey,
3, 24, Willyam Bradbury, 23

Note to Parents and Teachers

The All About Sharks set supports national curriculum standards for science related to the characteristics and behavior of animals. This book describes and illustrates goblin sharks. The images support early readers in understanding the text. The repetition of words and phrases helps early readers learn new words. This book also introduces early readers to subject-specific vocabulary words, which are defined in the Glossary section. Early readers may need assistance to read some words and to use the Table of Contents, Glossary, Read More, Internet Sites, Critical Thinking Questions, and Index sections of the book.

Table of Contents

Stretching Jaws

Deep in the ocean, it is dark. The slow goblin shark hides in the darkness. A squid swims by. Snap! The shark's jaws stretch out from its head and grab the squid.

Goblin sharks live in deep ocean waters. They mostly live between 885–3149 feet (270–960 meters) below the surface. These sharks live along the cold bottom of the ocean.

A Long Flat Snout

A goblin shark has a pinkish-white body. Its fins have a blue coloring. This shark has a long snout. Its tail fin is long too.

5 feet (1.5 meters)

8.5–12 feet (2.6 to 3.7 meters)

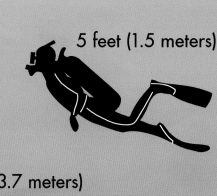

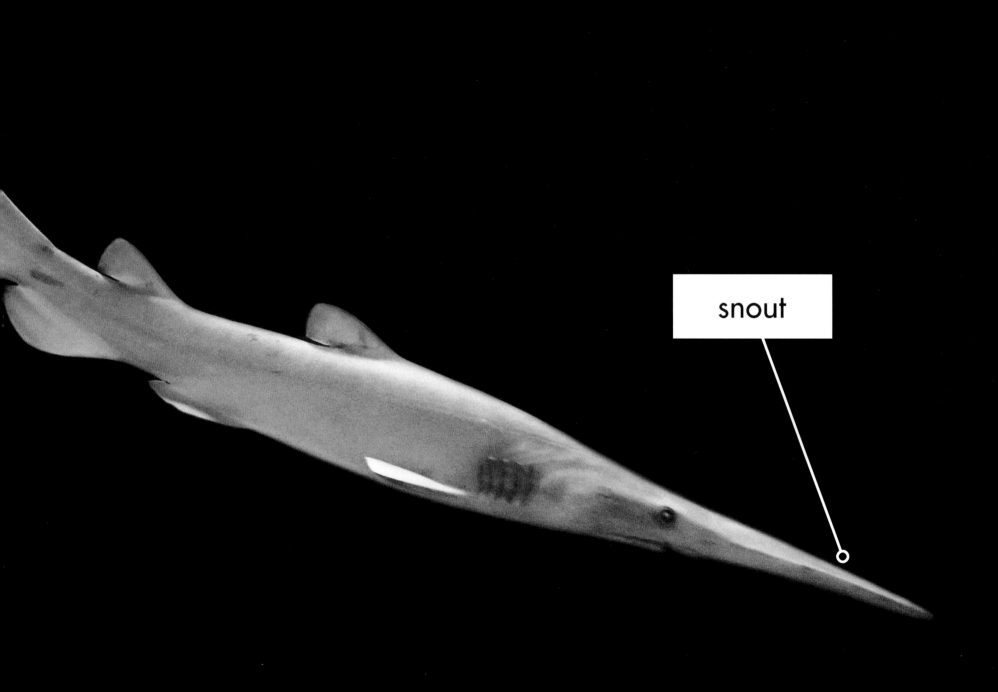

snout

There are five gills on each side
of the goblin shark's head.
Gills help it breathe in the water.

gills

The pectoral fins on a goblin shark are short and wide. These short fins are not made for quick swimming. Goblin sharks are slow swimmers.

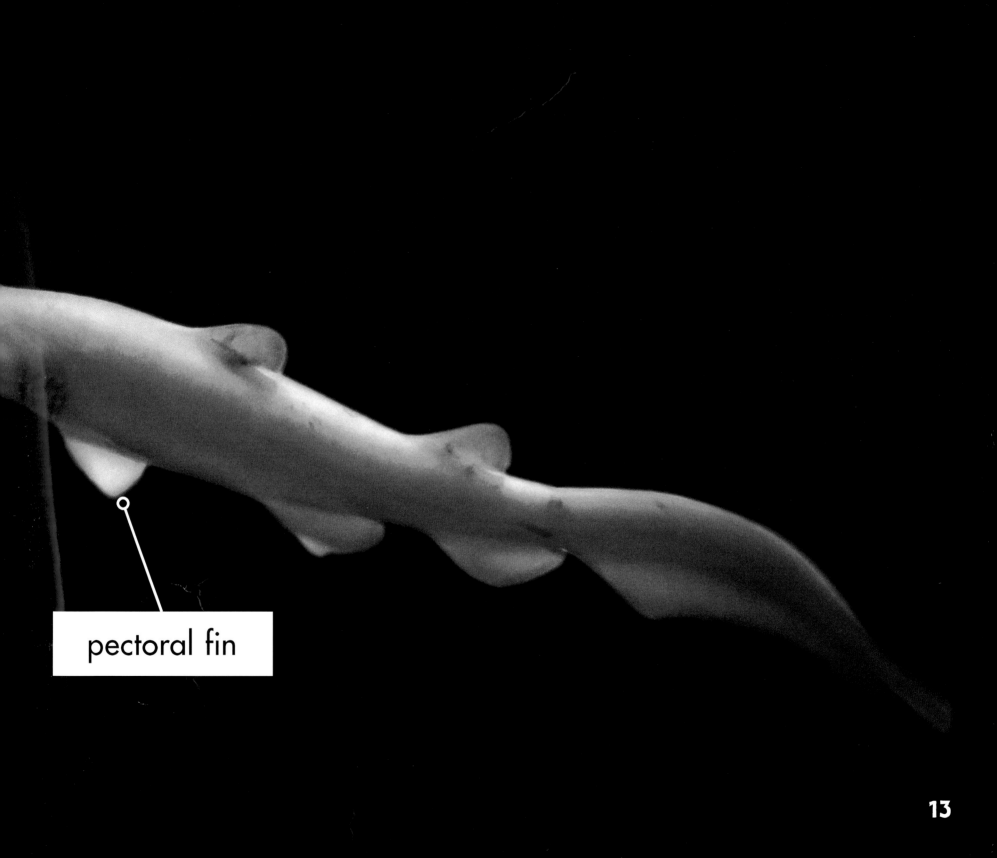

pectoral fin

A goblin shark's snout is long and flat. It has special organs that help the shark find food. These special organs can sense movement. This helps the shark find prey swimming nearby.

Hunting and Eating

Goblin sharks have long, skinny teeth that are very sharp. They eat fish, shrimp, and squid. They also eat octopus and crabs. Their flat back teeth can crush the crab's shell.

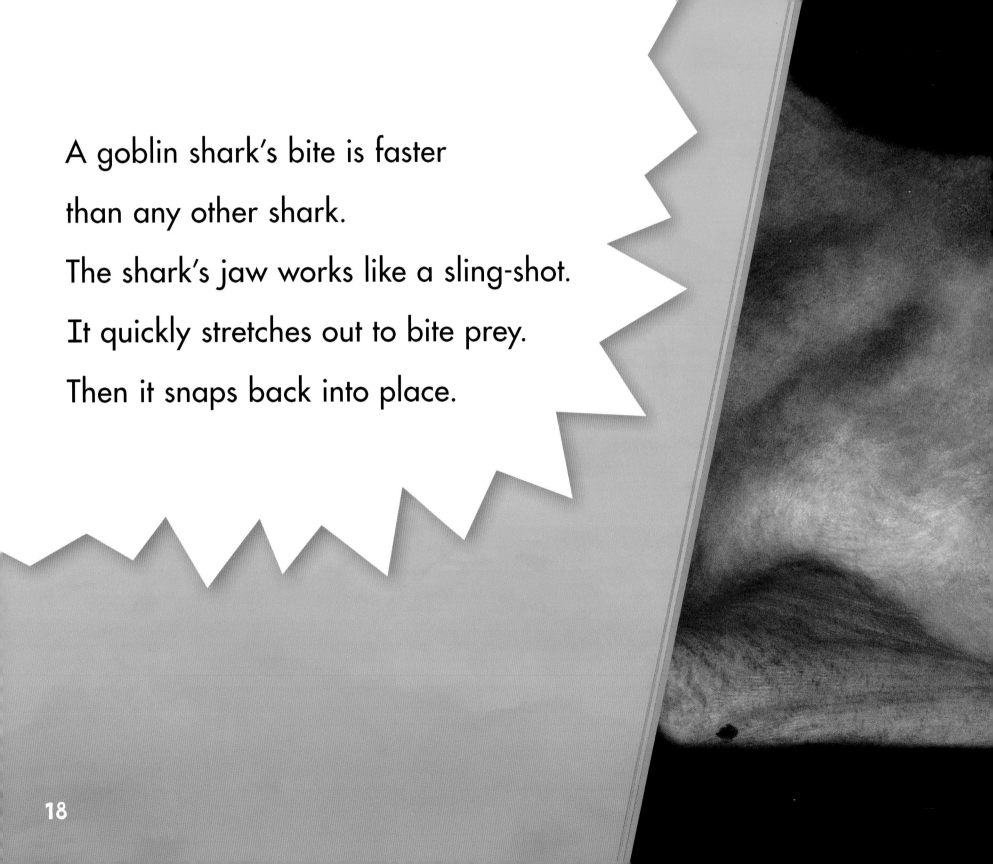

A goblin shark's bite is faster
than any other shark.
The shark's jaw works like a sling-shot.
It quickly stretches out to bite prey.
Then it snaps back into place.

Goblin Shark Babies

Not much is known about goblin shark pups. No one has ever seen one. No one knows exactly how long goblin sharks live.

Glossary

gill—a body part on the side of a fish; fish use their gills to breathe

organ—a body part that does a certain job

pectoral fins—a pair of fins on each side of the head

prey—an animal hunted by another animal for food

pup—a young shark

snout—the long front part of an animal's head; it includes the nose, mouth, and jaws

squid—a sea animal with a long, soft body and 10 fingerlike arms used to grasp food

surface—the outside or outermost area of something

Read More

Green, Sara. *The Goblin Shark.* Shark Fact Files. Minneapolis: Bellwether Media, 2013.

Mason, Paul. *World's Weirdest Sharks.* Wild World of Sharks. Minneapolis: Hungry Tomato, 2018.

Tracosas, L.J. *Sharks: Encounter the Ocean's Top 20 Fiercest Sharks.* Creature Files. Bellevue, Wash.: Becker & Mayer! Kids, 2018.

Internet Sites

FactHound offers a safe, fun way to find Internet sites related to this book. All of the sites on FactHound have been researched by our staff.

Here's all you do:

Visit *www.facthound.com*

Type in this code: 9781977101570

Super-cool stuff!

Check out projects, games and lots more at
www.capstonekids.com

Critical Thinking Questions

1. How do goblin sharks catch their prey?

2. What job does the goblin shark's snout help them with?

3. Why are goblin sharks not dangerous to humans?

Index